Pundemonium
VOL. 6

James E. Larson

Lefse Press—Agoura Hills, CA
Paperback ISBN: 979-8-9899576-0-6
eBook ISBN: 979-8-9899576-1-3
Title: *Pundemonium Vol. 6*
Author: James E. Larson
Digital distribution | 2024
Paperback | 2024

Dedication

The author dedicates this book to his loving family, wife Cindy, daughter Erica, and son Greg. They have had to listen to the author over the years trying out the various puns on them. They deserve recognition for enduring that pun-ishment.

Chapter One

Everybody knows about Isaac Newton sitting under an apple tree and discovering the laws of gravity. I don't know if this is true, but someone told me that a relative of his with the same last name acquired his fitting nickname by sitting under a fig tree and having a fig fall on him and him finding its fruit very delicious.

Most people know about the bicycle race known as "The Tour de France" which is held in France as you might suspect. Little known fact is that there are a couple of tailors that follow the riders around the course to repair any ripped uniforms. The tailors call their group "Tore de Pants!"

At a local dairy milk processing plant, they increased the conveyor speed that sends bottles of milk through the sterilization machine. The bottles of milk now go pasteurize so fast it is hard to see them.

A man opened up a horse beautician shop and claimed that if you bring your horse in, he would completely revitalize the long hair on the horse's neck. That was the shop's mane selling point.

All of a sudden, in the middle of a somewhat very long confusing speech that went on and on, the politician felt the effects of food poisoning but rather than stop the speech, he wambled on...

I know a guy who enjoyed talking about making things out of leather. He said he knew everything there was to know about the small pointed tool used for piercing small holes in leather like the narrow leather straps attached to wristwatches. He talked about the tool all the time but he never made anything out of leather.

He was awl talk and no action.

Chapter Two

Providing a delicious snack, which is the end result of dried grapes, is the grape's raison d'être!

In order to draw attention to a building supply store, the store began selling blue-colored sand in bulk. The store posted a picture of the sand with the store's advertising slogan, "Get A Load Of This!"

A vendor in Egypt was selling tickets to tour the Great Pyramid of Giza. He would sell you the tickets only after you had promised that two other people would buy tour tickets. The vendor then said you would get a small amount of money from those tickets. Sounds like he was starting to run a Pyramid Scheme.

The owner of a hair care line of products was considering adding a line of dandruff shampoos. After some thought, he realized he would be too exhausted to spend all the time needed to produce that dandruff product so in the end, he flaked out.

It seems there was another dance group I heard about that was formed by a group of old plumbers in London. Their favorite dance to perform was to the hit song, "Do the Lo-commode-tion!"

A candy company that made candy canes for the holidays recently added some new hip young people to their Board of Directors. The new young members of the board wanted to go in a healthier direction and so they wanted to add a new product for sale. That product was the same shape as the candy they had made for years but it was made out of dried grapes. They liked creating a disturbance on the board and it showed in the name of the product which was "Raison Cane!"

In the South, an elderly famous garden designer was being honored at a garden party in a garden she had designed which was full of her favorite plant the Laurel shrub. At the podium, she gave her thanks for the award and dropped the news that she was retiring. On the way back to her seat, she tripped and fell sitting down on top of one of her favorite plants. A bystander quipped, "Well, it looks like she is already resting on her Laurels!"

A factory that makes women's clothing all of a sudden just declared that they will not be producing "Pedal Pusher" type pants in the future. Many in the fashion industry called that a capricious statement!

In order to save some Birch Trees around a beaver pond near their town in Oregon, a member of the town council suggested laying out among the trees some flat low wood shipping items like the ones used by forklift operators. At first, no beavers touched them. Someone suggested sprinkling them with a light cheese salad dressing to make them more palletable.

Somebody asked a person why they love the game of charades so much. The person replied, "I think it goes without saying!"

I don't know if this is true or not, but I heard a long time ago in the 1800s that a group of wagon train pathfinders banded together to help settlers find new ways through the Oregon Trail. The pathfinders even had their own special jacket-like sport coats they wore that had a red stripe along their lapels. The Pathfinders got to be known as the "Trail Blazers!"

Chapter Three

At a factory that only made the metal bars that you put in a horse's mouth to control the direction of the horse, the workers heard rumors that their workload would increase because the factory would be making other things. The president tried to calm the workers down by telling them to just do their bit and that's all.

A company that produces percussion instruments for high school bands hired a marketing company to drum up some new business.

Two kings, who were brothers, ruled their kingdoms in Europe for a very long time and were also accomplished horsemen who enjoyed driving stagecoaches in their spare time. At that time, a servant had to sit on one of the lead horses to steer the horses. An inventor came up with the idea of running thin leather straps from the lead horse's mouth back to the driver of the stagecoach. The kings were thrilled with the new concept. The inventor, who was an admirer of the kings sent a note to both kings which said, "I hope you are enjoying your long reins!"

The marketing department at a champagne winery hired a stone sculptor to create a 20' tall bottle for a trade show. The sculpturer told the department he would carve it out of Quartz rock. The department said no and said, "Everybody knows champagne is never sold in Quartz!"

A cinematographer was working on a camera that would capture the full view of the horizon when he was filming. He was hoping the new camera would pan out.

Chapter Four

In the City of Athens in the Middle East, a small carnival had a bunch of trained monkeys that as part of their act would be working on a small car. The act was billed as "The Original Greece Monkeys!"

At a circus in New York, a group of dancers liked to perform on poles that allowed the dancers to be at a great height off the ground.

No matter how much they practiced, they still looked stilted.

I heard if you can't make ends meet, you should try making one a vegetable.

A famous author had in his contract with his publisher that he had to be present at the book factory when the books were produced and assembled. That part of the contract was binding.

Four people from a large furniture factory in Vermont decided to form a professional singing group. They decided they would only sing in local establishments where travelers could have lodging, food, and drink. Since they were all accountants at the factory, the name for the act they chose was, "The Inn Voices!"

In old England, two people in armor and on horseback would ride toward each other with their large lances pointed at each other trying to knock each other off their horses. You ask what time of day did the match start? Whenever it was, it was joust in time. When did the match end? When the knight fall occurred.

I guess some people who are natives of a country just don't like tourists. If you are a tourist being yelled at in France because you are wearing a French cap, are you being bereted?

Chapter Five

An art Teacher at a High School instructed his class that they would take a sheet of clear paper and put it over a photo of a person's head. The students would then draw lines found in the face of the photo below up onto the clear paper atop the photo. When the teacher told the students to begin, he noticed one student left the room. Looks like that student vanished without a trace.

There is a new book out now that explores the mysteries of acupuncture. It will also show you how to use it on yourself. That book will keep you on pins and needles.

The new owner of a roofing company, who just moved into a new office, was anxious to hang out his shingle.

At a cooking school, the students were in the middle of a test where they had to identify different types of meat. When called upon, they would have to pick up one of the meats arranged before them with a large tweezer-like kitchen utensil and name the type of meat. One student, when asked what type of meat he was holding said, "I know it but I can't remember its name...it's right on the tip of my tong!"

No matter how far you try to push the envelope, it will know when it is licked.

A patient at a dermatology office was itching to have his exam over with.

An inspector on the factory production line that was making A-framed small portable canvas-covered structures for camping noticed that the canvas covering was of low quality and he shut the line down. He said what he saw was a portent that could affect the company's sales.

Chapter Six

A young Priest in a rural church wanted to improve his congregant's communications skills. When his parishioners would confess their transgressions to him and they used incorrect sentence structures, he would fine them one dollar. One parishioner was not happy.

"This sounds like a syntax issue," he exclaimed!

A young boy was helping to make candy with his mother in their kitchen. His job was to take the long tweezer-like kitchen utensil and remove the candy from the candy sauce in a big bowl. The boy said he did not like licking the candy sauce off that kitchen utensil, although he was licking it while the utensil was in his mouth. His mother said he was saying that "tong-in-cheek!"

There was a recent robbery at a local plant nursery. The thieves got away with some strawberries. Those strawberries are now being considered as stolen merchandise.

A robber was caught in the act of stealing a toilet at a plumbing store. A clerk grabbed the tool you use to unplug a toilet and stuck the suction part of that tool over the robber's head. The robber was immediately plunged into submission.

A drama teacher, who was also a Zoologist, told his students to pick a wild animal and do a short-acting scene like that wild animal. Kathy, a student, chose a bear. "Ok," said the teacher to Kathy, "do ursine!"

A scientist interested in large ocean mammals was going to write a book on Orcas. He observed that a group of them easily took different roles when they were getting ready to hunt for food. He declared they were very good at what he called orcanizing.

Chapter Seven

An antique book dealer was selling the book "Walden-or-Life In The Woods." At the last moment, he decided to include another book by the same author in the same deal. The dealer thought that it would make a lot of sense to Thoreau those books together for sale.

For some unknown reason, somebody is doing a musical about Killer Whales. The producers are looking for someone to do the orca-stration.

The wife of a man was upset at him because he was writing a book about a small winged fly that resembled a mosquito. She said he was wasting his time on whatever that thing is called.
He replied, "It's gnat to me!"

The metal nail-like fasteners used to secure the railroad steel rails to the wooden ties was a very good solution and it began a spike in their use and it continues to this day....

I heard a former lumberjack found a way to make a jelly-like sandwich spread out of tree bark. He is calling his product "Log Jam!"

A car upholstery shop is requiring their employees during their fire safety drills to "Stop, Drop, Tuck and Roll!"

A witch wanted to join the Witches Association. The procedure requires the Association to send to the applicant's house two people to interview the applicant. They found she had a very huge boiling cauldron but her laugh was very ordinary. She was all vat and no cackle.

Chapter Eight

An inmate, who was an actor in a prison theater group, found an old prison guard uniform. He put it on, acted like he was a guard, and walked out of prison. Various people said that was his "breakout role!"

A small college in Hawaii had a student who graduated with great honors in the study of volcanoes. She was awarded the title of "Magma Cum Lava."

A husband was trying to decide to build the couples retirement home in the mountains or on the beach. He chose the beach because of the ocean breezes. When the wife was asked if that was his final decision, she said, "Yes, that's a shore thing!"

Do you think it is true that gophers are living on burrowed time?

A Mexican Pop singer, who was also a chef, did a cover version of an old Cindy Lauper song. The new cover version song is called, "Girls Just Want To Have Flan!"

I know a writer who only writes during the 8th month of the year. He said he wants to be known as an august writer.

A music composer working on a new song thought the song was going to be too long by two or three notes and they were to be sounded together in harmony. So after he "gave birth" to the song, he proceeded to cut the chord.

A sad story from a pet owner. A man who kept a pet parrot at his house saw his parrot fly into the unused fireplace and up the chimney where it just flue away....

Chapter Nine

A man went to a restaurant and his wife was going to join him later. He ordered his food and then ate so much that he texted his wife to tell her where he was in the restaurant. He texted, "I am sated next to the front door!"

A man was being interviewed by a reporter. The reporter asked him if he lives by any principles.

"Yes," said the man, "my next-door neighbor is one at a high school."

A store tried to sell paper and envelopes out of a panel truck but they had no success. I guess the lesson is the place where you sell your paper and envelopes should remain a stationary store.

A newspaper critic reviewed a lecture given by a man who talked about mountain climbing. The critic thought the man gave his peak performance.

A man invested money in a chain of butcher stores. He said he heard that was one way he would always have a steak in the business.

In Texas, a small community college was offering a couple of adult classes during the summer break. One class was sword fighting since the instructor used to teach actors how to fight with those weapons. The other class taught people how to build barriers on property lines to keep the neighbor's cattle separated. It seems no matter which class you signed up for, you would be doing some fencing.

A man begrudgingly went to an auto racing event with some of his friends. Just to be a little defiant, the man printed on the side of his face the words, "I Like Horse Racing More!" One of his friends that that was a bit cheeky!

Chapter Ten

J ust know that if you choose archaeology as a major in college you have a good chance that your career will end up in ruins.

An ocean shipping company constructed a new beautiful dock on the waterfront. Wouldn't you know it, a competitor constructed a beautiful dock right next to it. The competitor said he had to keep up with everybody, but he admitted it was basically pier pressure.

The oldest tea bag company in the world was steeped in history.

In Spain, a retired bullfighter was going to use some of his money to produce a TV game show. It was a knockoff of an American TV game show where people dress up in costumes but with a bullfighter theme to it. They were going to call it "Picador!"

A man went to a plastic surgeon to have his nose sculpted. When the bandages came off, he thought the nose was bigger than he thought it would be. The surgeon said he was sorry but he was hoping the patient could over look it.

Almost everyone knows Santa enjoys being outdoors in the fresh air delivering presents to the boys and girls. But someone told me he dislikes small confined spaces. He apparently suffers from "Claustrophobia."

A government official was giving a safety lecture at a small appliance factory that makes the appliance that presses out wrinkles in your clothes. After the lecture, while he was walking around the factory, he tripped and ended up kneeling on one of the appliances. The factory medical person said nothing serious happened but only said the person giving the safety lecture has suffered a mild case of "Irony."

Chapter Eleven

Surprisingly, in the Disney movie "Angels In The Outfield," angels help a baseball team win a game. The angels were just waiting in the wings.

At a large residential estate in New Jersey, two landscape maintenance companies were bidding on maintaining the landscape. After looking at the existing lawn which had many bare spots, company "A" gave the responsibility of caring for the lawn to company "B." Company "A" just thought that the lawn required just too much work and it needed to be ceded.

A kitchen utensil store in Iowa decided to have a sale on only ice cream utensils. They called a local reporter who came by and the reporter told them he would run that news in the paper. The store was so happy they told the reporter he could pick out any ice cream utensil for his keeping. His newspaper was pleased that their reporter got his scoop.

When are you not able to see a camel? The answer is when his "camelouflage" has been applied.

The plant manager at a small appliance factory that makes the appliance that presses the wrinkles out of clothes just received news that he would not be able to produce the number of appliances that the president of the company projected. That made the manager feel bad along with his other ailments like extreme fatigue, weakness, and headaches. No matter how you look at it, the manager was suffering from some sort of iron deficiency!

Chapter Twelve

A scientist was conducting an experiment about adding the life form that is a symbiotic partnership of two separate organisms, a fungus and an alga to the surface of a rock. A coworker asked him what he was doing in his experiment and what did he think of the result of it on the rock. The scientist said in answer to both of his questions, "I am lichen it."

A store in Australia that sells boomerangs tells their customers that if they are dissatisfied with their product, they can get their money back because the store has a 100% return policy.

The student actors at an acting school knew that when they practiced their tableau scenes, the acting school activity would be at a standstill.

The unpleasant person who was on a diet decided to quit his diet but he would still be off putting.

There was a strange endurance contest sponsored by a furniture factory in England. The contestants would see how long they would last in a chair that rocks back and forth. After a couple of hours, one contestant went a little crazy and proceeded to go off his rocker.

For a novelty reason, a pet store owner in a small rural town in Iowa has trained two doves to add the self-adhesive white powder onto Christmas trees during the holiday season. Wouldn't you know it, the local newspaper heard about it and published the headline "Birds of a Feather Really do Flock Together!"

On the History Channel, the old film of loading oats onto a ship was kind of grainy.

Chapter Thirteen

The British Army would not acknowledge that the color scheme of its newest tank was a dark gray-brown color. They said that information was taupe secret.

Young new board members wanted to shake things up at the company that makes the soft, cohesive substance designed to be chewed without being swallowed. They wanted to gum things up!

The numismatic speaker was only given five minutes to give a speech at the convention. He felt short-changed.

At the dress factory, when it came time to sew on the small, shiny, disc-shaped ornaments on the piece of clothing, it marked a change in the sequins of events.

When two card players heard about a rule change at their card club where they now can't play the popular one-man card game, they announced their solitairedy in denouncing the change.

The factory workers at a bathroom tissue plant were starting two-ply methods on the final product.

In a neighborhood, there was a string of robberies that were linked together because, at the site of the crimes, there were always footprints of somebody in bare feet. The police dubbed the suspect they caught "The Barefoot Bandit!" At trial, plaster casts of the footprints showed the burglar had no arches in his feet and they matched the plaster casts. The suspect was caught flat-footed.

Some people like to do things the old-fashioned way. Like when they still prefer to churn out butter.

Chapter Fourteen

The Architectural Critic of a large city's newspaper raved about the graceful curves of a new bridge and called it "Spantastic!"

As the dentist's very first patient sat in the dentist's chair, the very young and nervous dentist asked her to open her mouth and she did. Amazing, thought the dentist, here I am on my first day as a dentist and I already issued a jaw-dropping request.

A man wanted his money back from the company that sold him the digging tool that drills narrow deep circular holes in the ground. He said it was poorly made which does not augur well for his contractor crew.

Latest from the existing tilting large tower in Pisa, Italy. The owner of the tower has not been paying his bills to the maintenance crew of the tower, so the head of the maintenance crew is considering putting an additional lien on the tower.

The well-known arrogant actress was holding a lot of free promotional products given to her at the opening of a new store in Hollywood. At some point, all that free stuff caused her to swag out the front door.

I heard there was a new type of profession being offered in the capital city of Egypt. A member of this profession not only tells tourists about all the sites they should visit and how wonderful they are, but they also can adjust your spine and give you a massage. They are called Cairopractors.

The moonshiners' determination of what they thought just caused the big explosion at their campsite was that it was still up in the air.

Chapter Fifteen

A Magnet School in Los Angeles was known for teaching students about how human beings have changed over thousands of years. Their curriculum was always evolving.

A young doctor was assigned to a summer youth swimming camp on the East Coast. His office was right next to the camp's shallow water pool and he would have the kids stay in the pool until they would be called into his office. I guess they were all wadding to see the doctor.

I heard that the large famous company that grows many acres of pineapples in Hawaii often doles out free pineapple juice drinks in its visitor center.

A beach footwear company was shut down by the authorities in Florida because the owner failed to pay its property taxes for years and he was also using toxic rubber. Well, a new owner bought the company, paid the taxes, and is using the correct rubber. However, to capitalize on all the publicity surrounding the former owner, the new owner is selling his footwear bearing the name "Scandals!"

There is a dentist in the south who claims he can predict pretty accurately what will happen in the future to all the teeth in your mouth. He calls himself "The Toothsayer!"

The construction worker who was digging ditches with a hand tool was happy at the end of the day when he turned in his tool. He didn't mind a bit either about his scruffy appearance as he was dishoveled at the end of the day.

Chapter Sixteen

A thief snuck into a pet store and took off with two small puppies that happened to be very sick. The thief was caught and brought before the court. The judge charged the man with obtaining ill-gotten gains.

Two expert mountain climbers were arguing about who had climbed the tallest mountain. A wannabe climber heard them and told them when he hears people talk about mountains, his interest is always at its peak.

I heard, in a prison in upstate New York, that the warden prefers that the prisoners mix together in the exercise yard and play group card games that involve more than one person. If the warden catches anybody playing the card game you play by yourself, he will put you in solitary confinement.

A worker on a motion picture set who for over fifty years handled the rigging and equipment that supports the camera suddenly retired. He told everybody he was going to write a book about all the behind-the-scenes drama he has experienced over the years. A book critic said that will be a gripping book.

A confused young fisherman made a long pole with a barbed hook on the end. He wanted to sell it so he listed it in an advertisement in the paper as a harpoon. That wasn't true as he had just made a big gaffe.

33

Chapter Seventeen

The small old boxer had his face punched so many times in the past that his face looked like an old water bucket. When he went to the doctor because he did not feel well and had no color in his cheeks, the doctor said, "I think your face looks like it's a little pale!"

An orchestra leader was leading his orchestra when all of a sudden the light exploded that was shining light on his music score. Electricity flowed from the light through his body and up through his hand that had the metal baton. He quickly recovered. Newspapers the next day said it showed he was a good conductor.

Did you hear about the hot dog vendor at a baseball park who mustered up enough courage to ask his girlfriend to marry him? She said yes but she had to leave right away so she said to him to catch up with him later and they would celebrate. He said he would relish that.

An artist who paints with a support structure that the canvas frame rests on, helps the painter do his work easel-ly.

An old eccentric man on the beach in San Diego tells tourists that he has named all the long-winged web-footed white sea birds around him on the beach. For ten dollars from a couple, he will point to the bird and tell the tourists the name he has given it. The people who believe him are considered very gullible.

Do you want to know how to lose ten pounds quickly? Just throw 200 schillings into the Thames River.

Chapter Eighteen

A patient was going to have an operation at the hospital and he was asked by the doctor if the patient wanted to use an old-style anesthetic. The doctor said, "Ether you use it or you don't!"

A good furniture maker is looking at a piece of wood. If he sees the arrangement of the overall wood fiber pattern instead of the individual fibers and he is unsure if he should be doing that, then when he uses that piece of wood, he has to take it with a grain of gestalt.

I don't know if this story is true or not, but I heard a story about when the author of the Tom Sawyer book was giving a speech many years ago about his love of being around steam locomotives. Midway through the speech he forgot where he was in the speech. He had lost his Twain of thought.

The National Wood Classification Association, in an effort to be more inclusive with society as a whole, has come up with some guidelines on the naming of various wood items. For example, the upright wood supports for a house wall can be either called "studs" or they can now be called "hussy's" depending on your gender.

At the Tournament of Lumberjacks, one old event is where two men, with axes, have to make a tall tree fall. Other than that, there are no rules. They don't even have to clean up afterward. They just let the chips fall where they may....

Chapter Nineteen

I heard an interesting story about a zoo keeper in a small village in South America a long, long time ago who came up with a popular food dish. He discovered a small sluggish mammal tree dweller in his care just loved to be fed cabbage sliced into small pieces along with shredded carrots and onions and a creamy dressing. The public heard about it, tried it, liked it, and named it "colesloth" at the beginning.

A wealthy chef in France recently tried to buy up all of Europe's supply of dehydrated mixes of broth flavoring consisting of meat, fish, and vegetable flavors. In his thinking, if he had a monopoly on those dehydrated mixes, he could charge people a really high price. He admitted he is trying to become a bouillonare.

A boy was complaining about the breakup with his former girlfriend. They were both deep into Zodiac signs and it seems his "Lion" sign did not get along with her "Bull" sign. He said her sign "Taurus" apart.

An old store owner was planning to reduce the size of his shop and take life a little easier. He sold only instruments that measured the weight of different things. It made sense to him that he was going to scale back his inventory.

An employment ad was put in an Australian newspaper asking for someone to give talks at the Living History Exposition Building in Sydney. They wanted someone to give speeches about the native small grey fur mammal that eats plants and is usually found up in a Eucalyptus tree. An applicant went in for an interview and was asked what he knew about that animal. The applicant replied, "I have been studying that animal all my life! I think I have excellent Koalafications!"

Chapter Twenty

A small clothing store in Detroit, that only sold men's coats, was trying to get men interested in a new/old version of a man's coat. What the designer in the store did was take a lightweight coat that was designed to protect the wearer from rain/snow, was water-resistant, and reached down to the knees, and then he proceeded to remove the bottom half of the coat. They were sold as "Tranch Coats 2.0."

I heard there was a 400-pound native in the jungles of South America that sits around his hut eating with his hands T-Bone steaks all day. He tells anybody who will listen that he is really smart too. His fellow villagers just call him a "big-gnaw-it-all."

A wildlife veterinarian in Montana came up with a medicine to help a member of the deer family that is prone to upset stomachs. It is a tablet that fizzes when you put it in water and he is selling it under the name of "Elka-Seltzer."

Years and years ago, there was a department store in New York that employed orphans as young as seven to serve as elevator operators. That just seems wrong on so many levels....

Detectives today raided a booth at a county flea market for selling counterfeit decorative pillowcases. The detectives called the whole thing a sham operation.

In Norway, there were so many conflicting rules on how to fish for the popular North Atlantic Ocean fish that the Norwegian Fish Council decided that the rules had to be codified.

Chapter Twenty-One

The issue of people that give "word salad" answers to questions needs a dressing. Perhaps a dressing sticky enough to keep their mouths shut.

The Director of the American Sweet Potato Association was giving a long speech about all the advantages of eating sweet potatoes. He just kept on yammering.

I think it was the inventor Thomas Edison who came up with the quote "Genius is one percent inspiration and ninety-nine percent perspiration." So conversely, if you have no desire to be a genius, don't sweat it!

A very young preschool student stood before the blackboard. He was told to add up two figures but he was somewhat confused and could not add them up. Both he and the numbers on the board ended up nonplussed.

A daughter received from her father's estate a device upon which you can weave rugs. She was very pleased to receive her heirloom.

When Sir Isaac Newton developed his theory about the phenomenon of objects falling back on the ground after throwing them up in the air, he realized the "Gravity of the Situation."

The podiatrist said he didn't need any malpractice insurance because he said if he ever to sued he would call on his archangel.

Two young brothers were arguing about the rules to play "Hide and Seek." Their mother noticed one of the brothers didn't close his eyes when the other brother went and hid so they were irritating each other. So she laid down one of her rules that she thought would cover everything, which was "No piquing!"

An erratic violin player kept annoying his neighbors by playing his instrument until three o'clock in the morning. Police were called and he was told to stop doing that. The player said he would not stop. So the police took all his violin strings. That move took guts.

About the Author

The author, James E. Larson, has always enjoyed a good pun. Just recently, he decided to create new ones for a book. He says like anything else, some puns come easy while other need some rewrites before they are finished. A good pun needs a good back story that sets up the 'Pun-ch Line.' That is the fun part of creating puns.

9 7 9 8 9 8 9 9 5 7 6 0 6